Home Crafts

Home Crafts

A handy step-by-step guide

DK

LONDON, NEW YORK, MELBOURNE,
MUNICH, DELHI

Project Editor Katharine Goddard
Senior Art Editor Elaine Hewson
Managing Editor Penny Smith
Senior Managing Art Editor Marianne Markham
Producer, Pre-Production Rebecca Fallowfield
Senior Producer Katherine Whyte
Special Sales Creative Project Manager Alison Donovan

DK INDIA
Editors Janashree Singha, Manasvi Vohra
Senior Art Editor Balwant Singh
Art Editor Zaurin Thoidingjam
Assistant Art Editor Nikita Sodhi
DTP Designer Satish Chandra Gaur

First published in Great Britain in 2014
by Dorling Kindersley Limited
80 Strand, London WC2R 0RL

Material in this publication was previously published in:
Craft (2012) and The Girls' Book of Craft and Activities (2013)

A Penguin Random House Company

Copyright © 2012, 2013, 2014
Dorling Kindersley Limited

2 4 6 8 10 9 7 5 3 1
001 – 193358 – Jun/2014

This edition produced for The Book People Ltd,
Hall Wood Avenue, Haydock, St Helens, WA11 9UL

A CIP catalogue record for this book is available
from the British Library

ISBN 978-1-4093-6974-5

Printed and bound in China by Leo Paper Products Ltd.

Discover more at **www.dk.com/crafts**

Contents

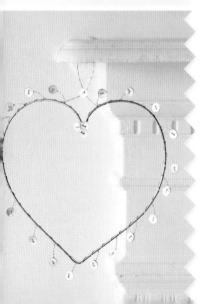

Introduction

BASKETRY • RAG RUGGING • NATURE CRAFTS • PRESSED FLOWER WORK

TINWORK• PAINTING FURNITURE • SOAP-MAKING • WIREWORK

Crafting can be really good for the soul – and it can also be extremely good for the planet. A project that uses materials that would otherwise be consigned to the bin means that there is less to dump in landfill sites and more to decorate your home. It's all about turning trash into treasures – so join the eco-craft revolution!

This book includes a range of crafts which make the most of natural or recycled materials. This is crafting with a conscience, the emphasis being on utilizing materials that might otherwise be thrown away.

Celebrating nature's bounty, by making baskets from stems of willow, a wreath from fresh and dried foliage, or a greetings card from pressed flowers could not be simpler. You may well be able to collect all the materials you need from a walk in the woods or from your own garden.

City dwellers who may not enjoy such easy access to nature may prefer to try the crafts that involve recycling. For instance, tin cans become candleholders and coat hanger wire is manipulated into a decorative, button-bedecked heart. Even crushed eggshells can be transformed into mini mosaics that breathe new life into an old picture frame.

For soaps, you'll almost certainly have some of the basic equipment and materials but you'll need to purchase certain items such as dyes and essential oils. Fortunately, there are plenty of suppliers, while online shopping brings these items within the reach of many people.

An unloved piece of furniture, destined for the scrapheap, can be revived and revitalized with a lick of paint and a couple of new knobs, or with a little hooking and prodding, a rag bag of scraps can be turned into a comfy rug.

Before you embark on any of the projects in this book, read through the instructions carefully, make a checklist of the items you need, and be sure to follow the safety guidelines.

Tools and materials

The great thing about crafting using old, recycled, or found materials is that they're free! You'll only need to invest in a handful of specialist tools, depending on which projects you make. A rummage in old storage boxes can unearth all sorts of treasures that can be turned into beautiful home decorations.

Basketry

Brown willow This type of willow is dried with its bark on. It needs to be soaked for several days so that it is flexible enough to use.

Bodkin This metal tapered spike is useful for making spaces in weaving. If you don't have one, use a metal skewer or screwdriver instead.

Buff willow Buff willow has been boiled and stripped. It becomes pliable after much less soaking than brown willow, so is handier if you don't have much time.

String Use this to tie the ends of a basket while you weave and to hold the shape of a basket after removing it from the former.

Compass This will help draw circles and semicircles to make a cardboard former. Measure the required radius on a ruler. For instance, a 15cm (6in) diameter circle will need a radius of 7.5cm (3in).

Side cutters These are needed to trim the willow accurately and closely. Garden secateurs can also be used, so long as they are sharp.

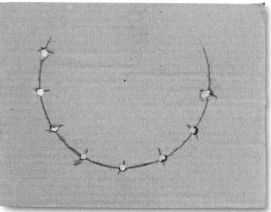

Former A former holds the willow stakes in shape while you weave. It can be made to suit whatever size structure you are making. Punch holes in a piece of cardboard then feed the willow through the holes.

Rag rugging

Recycled textiles In true keeping with rag rugging, textiles should be recycled: old T-shirts, fine-knit woollens, cotton sweatshirts, wool blankets, and old cotton sheets are all good. Heavy curtain material and fabrics that fray are unsuitable.

Hessian 10oz common hessian forms the base of the rug. It has an open weave and is easy to work on. You could also use jute grain sacks or coffee sacks.

Cutting gauge Used for cutting even tabs of fabric from a long strip.

Felt-tip pen Chalk out your design on the hessian and when you are happy with it, go over it with a felt-tip pen to make the lines clear.

Rug hook This brass rug hook with a bulbous yew handle is used for creating a hooked, looped pile.

Bodger With a pointed end and sprung jaws, this tool can grab short tabs of fabric so they can be pulled through hessian to create a proddy, clipped pile.

Embroidery hoop Used to stretch hessian taut to make rug hooking easier. Alternatively, you could use a tapestry frame.

Strong thread Use jute thread and strong button or carpet threads to securely stitch worked pieces of hessian together.

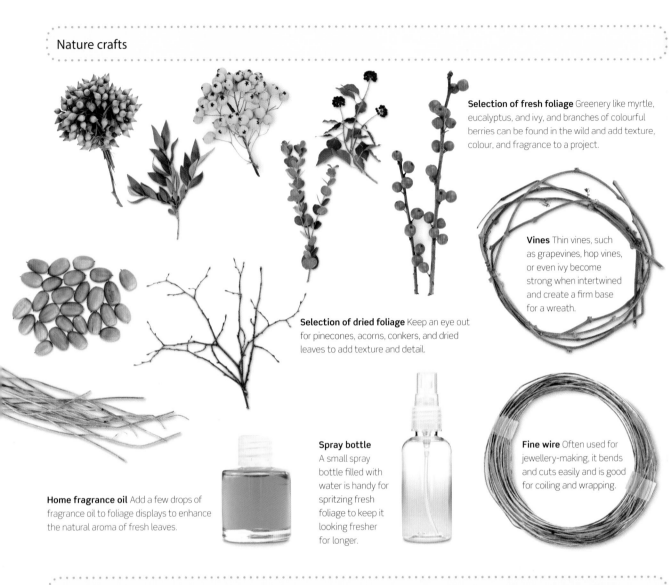

Nature crafts

Selection of fresh foliage Greenery like myrtle, eucalyptus, and ivy, and branches of colourful berries can be found in the wild and add texture, colour, and fragrance to a project.

Vines Thin vines, such as grapevines, hop vines, or even ivy become strong when intertwined and create a firm base for a wreath.

Selection of dried foliage Keep an eye out for pinecones, acorns, conkers, and dried leaves to add texture and detail.

Spray bottle A small spray bottle filled with water is handy for spritzing fresh foliage to keep it looking fresher for longer.

Fine wire Often used for jewellery-making, it bends and cuts easily and is good for coiling and wrapping.

Home fragrance oil Add a few drops of fragrance oil to foliage displays to enhance the natural aroma of fresh leaves.

Pressed flower work

Air-dry press Made of open-density foam with cotton layers onto which the flowers are placed, this press is held together with plastic mesh and Velcro straps. Warm air must be allowed to pass through the press in order for the flowers to dry in a day or two.

Traditional press This is made of sheets of newspaper separated by layers of smooth cardboard and held together by plywood boards secured with wing nuts. The flowers are placed between paper tissues or blotting paper, which are then placed between the newspaper layers. Left in a warm place, the flowers should be dry within a week or two.

Microwave press Two layers of felt with two cotton layers in between are held together with two microwavable plastic boards and clips. (The flowers are placed between the cotton layers and microwaved). They are pressed and ready to use in seconds. There are two sizes: 12.5cm (5in) and 27.5cm (11in) square.

Desiccant pads press Consists of a number of desiccant pads between which the flowers are placed on paper tissues. The pads lie between polystyrene boards held together with elastic bands. The flowers will be dry in a few days. After removing the flowers, the pads should be dried before reuse.

Card Obtain the best-quality card for optimal results. The card should be 225 to 260gsm to ensure it stands up when the flowers are attached.

Rubber-based glue Use a rubber-based glue; water-based glues will reintroduce moisture into the pressed and dried-out flowers. This will cause discolouration over time.

Furniture painting

Primer undercoat This seals the wood and forms an opaque base coat in preparation for painting with satinwood or eggshell.

Matt emulsion paint This is applied over primer undercoat on areas to be painted or stencilled. It provides a better surface for painting than primer undercoat alone. Finish with two coats of varnish.

Satinwood/eggshell Satinwood or eggshell is a top coat applied to furniture and interior woodwork. It has a contemporary, mid-sheen finish. Two coats are usually required.

Quick-dry water-based varnish This varnish is transparent and colourless. It is painted over the parts of furniture that have been stencilled or painted to protect against spills and knocks. Two coats are recommended.

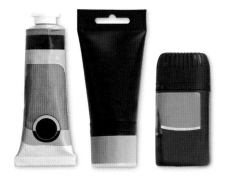

Scalpel This knife is very sharp and must be used with care. It is the easiest and most accurate way to cut designs from stencil card. Alternatively, you can use a craft knife.

Wood filler Used for filling small dents and gaps in wood. It can be sanded flat when dry.

Acrylic paints and/or sample pots of emulsion These are used to apply designs to furniture using stencils or paintbrushes. They can be mixed together to produce more colours.

Stencil brushes A stencil brush is short and stubby with firmly packed bristles. The stiff bristles reduce the chance of paint seeping under the stencil.

Stencil card Stencil card is oiled, heavyweight, and water-resistant. Designs are cut out of the card to create images which can be applied with a stencil brush to furniture, walls, and accessories.

Woodcare paintbrushes These brushes are used for painting and varnishing the body or the shell of furniture. The smaller sizes are useful for hard-to-reach areas.

Small artist's paintbrushes Brushes intended for use with watercolour and gouache paints are most suitable. Choose round brushes with sable or synthetic hairs. They are used for painting designs onto furniture and adding detail to stencilled designs.

Medium-grade sandpaper and sanding block Sandpaper is used for smoothing bare wood, removing varnish or old paint, and for sanding between coats of paint. When sanding a flat surface, it is more efficient to use the paper wrapped around a sanding block.

Tinwork

Tin cans These are actually not made of tin – they are sheet steel with a thin tin plating. Cans with a ring pull are ideal as they leave the rim intact and smooth.

Masonry nails These nails are hardened so they are an ideal choice for punching through a tin can.

Sandbag If you don't have a suitable fabric bag, a piece of heavy fabric will suffice – place sand in the centre, draw up the sides, and close with a cable tie.

Hammer Find a hammer that is comfortable to hold, but not too light. The weight of the hammer should do the work, rather than your arm.

Wirework

Small bolt cutters These are ideal for cutting through heavy wire – if you don't have bolt cutters, the built-in wire cutters on general-purpose pliers will do the same job.

Wire coat hangers These are made from relatively thick wire, which can be uncoiled and used for any craft project requiring wire.

Wire cutters Basic side-cutting wire cutters snip through thin- and medium-gauge wire.

Gardening gloves Wear gardening or thick fabric gloves when using wire to help you shape it more easily and protect your hands from sharp ends.

Cable cutters These are more robust than wire cutters and can cut through thicker wire, such as the type used for coat hangers.

Ring-bending pliers These have smooth jaws to minimize marks left on the wire, and have one curved and one flat jaw, which makes them ideal for bending heavy-gauge wire into a smooth, even curve.

Small mole grips Also known as vice grips, these are ideal for bending wire into straight lines or sharp angles. They can be adjusted so that they lock onto the item that you are gripping.

Medium-gauge wire A thinnish wire that bends and cuts easily and is good for coiling, wrapping, and joining wire ends together.

Soap

Teaspoon or beaker For measuring out quantities of essential oil or fragrance.

Melt-and-pour soap base These clear or opaque glycerine bases are designed for melting and re-moulding into bars.

Pans You can use any type of pan; just make sure the heatproof bowl fits neatly on top without touching the bottom of the pan.

Kitchen scales Electronic or old-fashioned kitchen scales both work well. These are used for weighing out the soap and other ingredients.

One or more heatproof bowls These are used for melting the soap, either on the hob or in the microwave.

Moulds These can be anything from fancy soap moulds to sturdy margarine tubs. Silicone bakeware and Tupperware are also ideal. Avoid anything that is liable to warp with heat.

Chopping board Chop the soap base into cubes on a plastic or wooden board.

Cocktail sticks These are handy for transferring dyes and pigments to the soap base in tiny increments.

Colourants Cosmetic pigments, dyes, and micas (powdered minerals) offer a safe and lasting way to colour soap. Food colours can also be used but are prone to fading so are best avoided.

Botanical additives Dried flower petals or buds, herbs, and dried fruit slices can add decorative interest to soaps. (Note that some ingredients, such as rose petals, will fade when embedded within the soap and are best kept as surface decoration. Dried calendula petals, on the other hand, will retain their vibrant colour when stirred into the soap.)

Metal scraper or knife Ideal for slicing soap into chunks and bars.

poppy seeds

honey

French green clay

ground
oatmeal

shea butter

Texture enhancers Finely ground oatmeal, honey, powdered clays, and solid oils and butters can all be used to add exfoliating or skin-conditioning properties to soap.

YOU WILL ALSO NEED...

Microwave oven For melting small quantities of soap (as an alternative to melting on the hob).

Rubbing alcohol or surgical spirit A liquid used for removing surface bubbles and helping soap layers to adhere to each other. Pour into a small spray bottle for easy use.

Metal spoons For stirring the melted soap.

Cling film For storing finished soaps that are not for immediate use.

Scents Essential oils are ideal for creating aromatherapy soaps, while synthetic fragrances offer a range of additional scent options. Only use essential oils or fragrances that are safe for cosmetic use.

Basketry TECHNIQUES

Willow is a beautiful material to use in basketry, but you need to follow some simple guidelines for its preparation and handling. Once you've learned the basics, you can experiment with making different-sized baskets and work with more complicated weaves.

Selecting materials

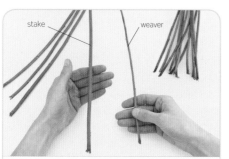

The stakes and weavers should be even in length and thickness. The stakes form the framework for the basket and the weavers weave around them. The stakes should be selected from a 5ft bundle of willow; the weavers from a 3ft bundle of willow. The thick end of the willow is called the butt; the thin end is called the tip.

Soaking and mellowing the willow

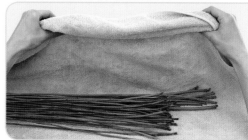

Willow is brittle when dry, so must be soaked by totally submerging it in cold water to make it pliable. After soaking, mellow the willow by wrapping it in a damp towel and leaving it overnight in a cool place to rest.

CALCULATING WILLOW SOAKING TIME

Buff willow has been boiled and stripped, so takes less time to soak than brown willow. Soak buff willow for 1 to 2 hours in cold water. Soak brown willow in cold water for one day per foot of willow (so 3ft willow will need to be soaked for three days). If you need to speed up the soaking time, use hot tap water and soak for a shorter time.

Making a cardboard former and framework

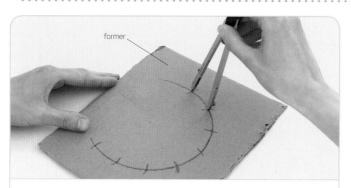

1 A former is used to hold the willow frame in the desired shape. Using a compass, draw an extended semicircle 15cm (6in) in diameter on a piece of cardboard, or draw around a plate of a similar size. Mark eight equally spaced points around the circumference. The points should be 3.5cm (1⅜in) apart.

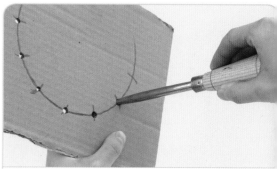

2 Make a hole through each point on the cardboard using a bodkin or skewer.

3 Before you feed the willow stakes through the holes to make the framework, cut a sharp angle across the butt end of the stakes using side cutters to help feed them through more easily.

Basic weaving

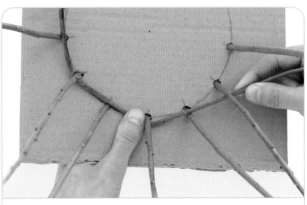

The weaving is worked by threading a weaver in front of one stake and behind the next. Each row of weaving should sit in the opposite place to the previous row. Use thicker weavers where the spaces between the stakes are big, and finer weavers as the spaces between the stakes become smaller.

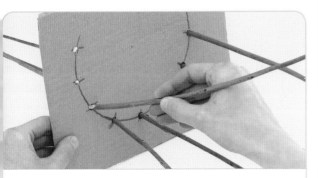

4 Push the first stake, butt end first, through the first hole until it is one-third of the way through. Push the next stake, butt end first, through the next hole from the other side of the cardboard until two-thirds of the stake is through. Continue pushing the stakes in alternately until they are all in place and the frame is completed. The ends should line up as a butt then tip, a butt then tip, and so on.

Weaving around the edges

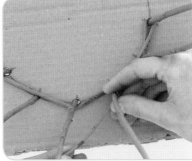

1 You can weave around the end stake by simply twisting the weaver around the stake and then weaving it back in the opposite direction.

5 Tie one end of the stakes securely with a length of string to hold them securely in place.

2 To make a more secure edge, wrap the weaver tightly around the end stake twice before weaving it back in the opposite direction. This ensures the weaver holds the stakes tightly.

Joining weavers

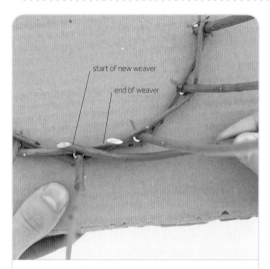

start of new weaver

end of weaver

1 When you finish with a butt end, join in a new weaver by placing a new butt in the next space. Continue weaving with the new weaver. Leave the butt ends inside; they will be trimmed at a later stage.

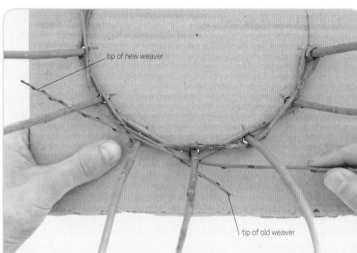

tip of new weaver

tip of old weaver

2 When you finish with a tip, lay the tip of the new weaver over the old weaver so that they overlap and run together for a short distance. Continue weaving with the new weaver.

Finishing off

1 Always finish weaving a basket with a tip, tucking its end away under the previous row of weaving.

2 Trim away any ends using side cutters, making sure that each weaver rests on a stake. When the willow dries out it shrinks a little, so ensure you leave the weaver a little on the long side. You can trim it back further when it has completely dried.

Binding stakes

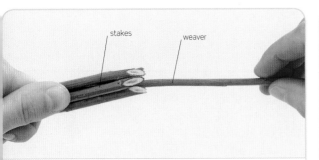

stakes   weaver

1 Binding is a method of tying the stakes of a basket together to make the framework secure. This is done after the weaving is complete. Trap the butt end of a weaver between the ends of the bunch of stakes, with the tip of the weaver pointing outwards.

90° angle

2 Bend the weaver at a 90° angle, making sure that the butt end of the weaver is held firmly between the stakes.

3 Wrap the weaver around the bundle of stakes, keeping plenty of tension.

4 Continue wrapping the weaver until there are five rows of binding, each sitting alongside the next.

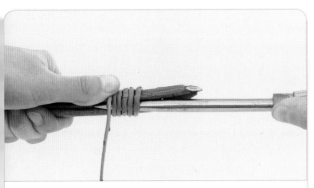

5 Holding the binding securely in place, use the bodkin to make a small space under the binding.

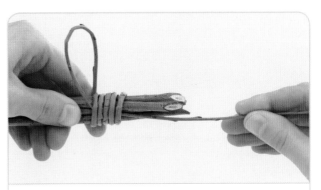

6 Remove the bodkin and feed the tip of the weaver underneath the rows of binding and back out in the direction it was originally pointing. Pull tightly to secure.

Willow fruit basket PROJECT

This quick and simple project uses brown willow to make a frame basket. The basket is woven around a cardboard former which holds the basket in shape while you concentrate on the weaving. Once you've mastered the basic weave you can enjoy watching the piece take shape. This basket makes a great fruit basket or looks good as a sculptural piece hung on a wall.

YOU WILL NEED

- stakes: 8 thick rods of 5ft brown willow
- weavers: 60 rods of 3ft brown willow
- towel
- side cutters
- cardboard former (see pp.18-19)
- compass
- string
- scissors
- ruler
- bodkin

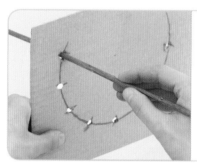

1 Soak and mellow the stakes and weavers, as shown on p.18. Push a stake through the first hole of the former, butt end first, until one-third of the stake is through. Push the butt end of the next stake through the next hole from the other side of the cardboard until two-thirds of it is through. Continue pushing the stakes in alternately until all eight are in place and the frame is completed. Tie the stakes together at one end with string.

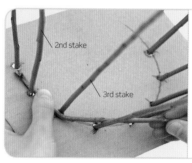

2nd stake

3rd stake

2 Begin weaving the untied side: place the butt of a weaver between the second and third stakes. Weave it in front of one stake, then behind the next. Wrap the weaver tightly around the last stake twice, then continue weaving in the opposite direction.

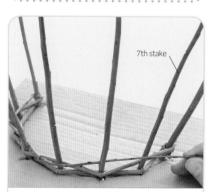

7th stake

3 Repeat until the weaver has travelled back and forth three times across the stakes, finishing on the opposite side to where it started. The tip of the weaver should sit on the outside of the seventh stake.

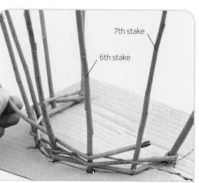

7th stake

6th stake

4 Place the butt of the next weaver between the seventh and sixth stakes and weave it across in the same way.

5 Continue weaving. Join in a new weaver at the opposite side of the basket to the last one. After weaving in six weavers, tie the ends of the stakes together with string to form a tapered end.

6 Continue weaving until there is about 15cm (6in) of weaving. Untie the ends of the stakes when they are too close to weave between.

7 Remove the cardboard former and tie string across the centre of the basket to hold the shape. Weave the second half of the basket in the same way as the first.

8 Bind the ends as shown in **binding stakes** on p.21. Trim any ends using the side cutters. Remove the string.

Rag rugging TECHNIQUES

This traditional craft is a great way to recycle fabrics. Use long strips of fabric worked onto a backing of hessian with a rug hook to create a dense, looped pile. To create a shaggy, clipped pile, pull shorter tabs of fabric through the hessian using a bodger.

The hooking technique

Preparing the fabric

Using a rug hook

2-3cm (³⁄₄-1¹⁄₄in) wide strips

Cut strips as long as the fabric allows. For speed, fold the fabric over and cut through the layers. The strips should be 2 to 3cm (³⁄₄ to 1¹⁄₄in) wide, depending on the thickness of the fabric. Generally, the thicker the fabric, the narrower the width of the strip.

1 Secure a piece of hessian in an embroidery hoop, ensuring the hessian is taut. Mark out your design, first in chalk and then, when you're happy with it, go over the lines with a felt-tip pen.

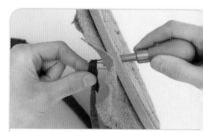

2 Hold the hook in one hand and the fabric strip in the other, under the frame. Following the design, push the hook into the hessian and catch the end of the strip in the hook.

3 Pull the end up through the hessian to about 2.5cm (1in) above the surface. It will be snipped off later to the height of the loops. Release the strip from the hook.

first loop

end of strip

4 Push the hook down into the hessian again three threads forwards, and pull a loop of fabric up to about 2cm (³⁄₄in) above the surface. Repeat, creating even loops, until you reach the end of the strip of fabric.

5 To start a new strip, push the hook down into the hessian where the end of the last strip came out. Pull up the end of the new strip. Allow about three threads of hessian between each row.

6 Carefully snip off the strip ends so that they are level with the loops.

The proddy technique

Preparing the fabric

1 Cut your chosen fabric into 2cm (¾in) wide strips. For speed, you can fold the fabric over several times and cut through the layers.

2 For this technique, you need tabs of fabric about 7.5cm (3in) long. To make these, wind a long strip of fabric around a cutting gauge, then cut along the groove using scissors.

Using a bodger

1 Mark your design on a piece of hessian using a felt-tip pen.

2 Following the design, push the pointed end of the bodger down into the hessian and back up two or three threads forwards, to create a "double hole".

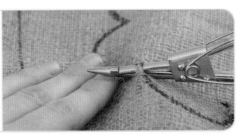

3 Open the jaws of the bodger, grab a tab of fabric by its end, and pull it halfway though the two holes. Release the tab.

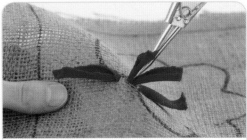

4 Push the bodger into the last hole made, bring it out two or three threads forwards, and grab the next tab of fabric.

5 Repeat, leaving two or three threads between each adjacent row of fabric. Set the stitches slightly further apart if you're using fluffy fabric as this will splay out, covering a greater area.

25

Rag rug mat PROJECT

The shaggy pile of this rag rug was made using the proddy technique, with wool and cotton recycled fabrics. Six small squares are made and then joined together, creating a wonderfully tactile and functional rug that would be ideal for the bedside, doorway, or in front of a fireplace.

YOU WILL NEED

- six 26cm (10¼in) squares of 10oz common hessian
- ruler
- felt-tip pen
- cardboard templates: 20cm (8in) square, with circle, heart, and flower shapes to fit within the square
- fine-knit recycled woollens and cottons in reds, greens, blues, greys, black, and purple
- cutting gauge
- scissors
- bodger
- glass-headed pins
- strong thread or jute thread
- sack needle

1 Using a felt-tip pen, mark each piece of hessian with a 20cm (8in) square. Within each square, draw either a circle, heart, or flower, using the cardboard templates. You can make two squares of each design or vary the design according to your own taste.

2 Prepare the fabrics, cutting them into tabs 2cm (¾in) wide and 7.5cm (3in) long. Following the **proddy technique** on p25, use the bodger to create a proddy pile on each hessian square.

3 Continue in this way, working on one square at a time and using different coloured strips to make a pleasing design, until you have completed all six squares, right to the marked edges.

4 When you have worked all the squares, turn each square to the wrong side and turn a double-hem in the unworked hessian along all four sides. Fold the hem into neat mitres at the corners. Pin and hand stitch using strong thread or jute thread.

5 Lay out the squares face down in a three-by-two rectangle and pin the hemmed edges together. Using strong thread or jute thread, sew the squares together to create the complete rug.

Nature crafts TECHNIQUES

Working with natural foliage provides the perfect excuse to go for a walk in your local park woodland, or forest – or you may even find suitable greenery in your garden. Look out for items that have fallen off trees, such as pine cones and acorns. Using fresh cuttings of berrie and firs creates a lovely seasonal aroma, or you can enhance the natural fragrance with a few drops of an appropriate fragrance oil.

Making a wreath frame

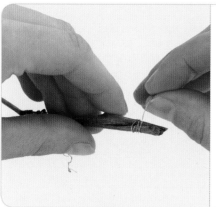

1 Strip two equal lengths of vine of their leaves. Secure them together by binding with a short length of fine wire.

twisted vines

2 Twist the vines together to make one strong length. Secure the other end with wire.

3 Bring the two ends together to create a circle. Twist the ends around each other and tie them together with a short length of wire. If the vines are too long, overlap the ends; if they're too short, introduce an additional length.

4 To strengthen the frame, add more lengths of stripped vine. Tie one end to the frame with wire and wind the vine around the frame, securing the other end with wire. Repeat until you have a strong, firm frame.

5 To keep the shape even and strengthen the frame more, tie small pieces of wire at regular intervals around the frame.

Working with fresh foliage

1 Ensure each stem of foliage is fresh, clean, and dry, and check it looks healthy. Avoid using materials that are mouldy as the mould may spread.

2 Use a sharp pair of scissors to trim foliage to the required size. For thick stems, use a pair of secateurs. These specialist gardening scissors can cut through branches up to 2cm (³⁄₄in) thick.

Making fir bunches

Use a sharp pair of scissors to trim the sprigs of fir to 4cm (1¹⁄₂in) lengths. Take small bunches of fir (about five sprigs) and wind a length of wire around the bottom of their stems to hold them together.

Securing foliage to the frame

1 To secure fresh foliage such as fir bunches to the frame, use a short length of wire to wrap the base of the bunch to the frame.

2 Use superglue to attach dried foliage, cones, and other material. Apply a dot of glue to the base of the item and then press in place, making sure not to glue any other foliage together.

Keeping foliage fresh

Fresh foliage should last for several weeks, though will wilt more quickly if it is left outdoors without shelter from the wind. Spritz it regularly with a fine mist of water to keep it fresh.

Enhancing the fragrance

Add a few drops of fragrance oil to fresh or dried foliage to enhance the natural fragrance.

Evergreen wreath PROJECT

Wreaths are a great introduction to floristry, giving you a chance to work with both fresh and dried foliage. Here, bunches of fir create the base for the frame, and pine cones, acorns, and colourful berries are dotted around to add texture and colour. You could also add leaves, dried fruits, and nuts to create a design that is unique and smells gorgeous.

YOU WILL NEED

- stripped vine stems
- scissors or secateurs
- fine wire
- selection of fresh foliage (fir sprigs, myrtle, berries, eucalyptus leaves)
- measuring tape
- selection of dried foliage (pine cones, acorns)
- superglue
- hook or ribbon
- fragrance oil (optional)
- spray bottle

1 Follow **making a wreath frame** on p.28 to make a 30cm (12in) diameter circular frame. Around six rounds of vine will make a thick, sturdy frame.

2 Follow **making fir bunches** on p.29 to make 15 to 20 bunches. Attach each one to the frame with wire so that they face the same direction. Overlap one bunch with the next to cover the entire frame.

measuring tape

3 Trim the remaining fresh foliage to size and arrange it around the wreath. Play with the design until you are happy with it before securing the foliage in place. Use a measuring tape to check that the spacing between the foliage is even.

4 Tuck individual sprigs of fresh foliage into the frame between the fir bunches. Attach other bunches of foliage with short lengths of wire, tucking the ends of the wire into the fir to hide them.

5 Arrange the dried foliage on top of the wreath to get an idea of the finished look, then glue in position.

6 Hang the wreath on a hook, or if you prefer, attach a ribbon at the top to hang it. You can scent it with a few drops of fragrance oil or leave it as it is. Spritz regularly with water to keep it fresh.

Pressed flower work TECHNIQUES

Follow a few basic principles and you'll find that pressed flower work can be most enjoyable. Flowers that press well and keep their colour include roses, buttercups, forget-me-nots, daisies, hydrangeas, and larkspur. Once you have more experience, you'll be able to press almost any plant material and achieve good results, though pressing fleshy flowers such as hyacinths and sedums may be more challenging.

Making a flower press

YOU WILL NEED

- 2 (5-ply) 15 x 20cm (6 x 8in) plywood boards
- 50 sheets newspaper cut into 15 x 20cm (6 x 8in) pieces
- 4 pieces 15 x 20cm (6 x 8in) smooth cardboard, 1.5mm ($^1/_{14}$in) thick
- 3 elastic bands, or 2 clamps, or 4 wing nuts and bolts

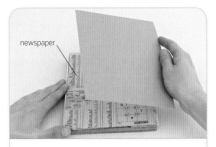

newspaper

1 To assemble the press, place one plywood board on the work surface and top with 10 sheets of newspaper. Place a thick piece of cardboard on top. Repeat the layers until you have sufficient layers for the flowers you wish to press.

plywood board

2 Position the other plywood board on top to finish the sandwich. Hold the press together with elastic bands, clamps, or wing nuts and bolts. (If using bolts, you'll need to drill two holes either side of the plywood boards to accommodate the bolts.)

Pressing using other devices

paper tissue

Flowers may also be pressed between paper tissues in the pages of a heavy book. Place the book in a warm place to ensure the flowers will dry in one to two weeks. Other flower presses are available (see pp.10).

Choosing flowers and leaves

Only press perfect specimens and make sure you press more than you'll need as some petals and leaves will inevitably get damaged when you handle them.

CONSERVING FLOWERS AND LEAVES

To ensure flowers remain in excellent condition, pick them on a dry day and put into the press straight away.

Warmth and low humidity are essential when pressing flowers. These conditions help to remove the moisture content quickly from the plant material and keep the colours vibrant.

Pressing flowers and leaves

1 Place the flowers and leaves in the press between layers of paper tissues or other smooth, white absorbent paper, such as blotting paper. Don't use kitchen paper (you'll end up with dimpled petals) or newsprint (the ink will mark the petals and leaves). Put flowers of a similar thickness on the same page in the press. This will produce an even pressure when drying.

2 Small flowers may be pressed whole but larger ones, such as some roses, gerberas, and peonies must be taken apart and pressed petal by petal. Reassemble them when dry.

3 Large flowers, such as freesias, may be cut through the middle before pressing to produce two flowers from one.

4 As soon as the flowers are dry, remove them from the press using tweezers. If they are not being used straight away, store them flat, in a dry place, in clearly labelled envelopes.

Glueing flowers and leaves to card

dot of glue

Dip the tip of a cocktail stick into a rubber-based glue and dot onto the back of a flower or leaf before placing onto card. Use just enough glue to hold the flower in position.

Sealing the work

1 If you're framing your work, seal it under a sheet of glass or acrylic; if you're making jewellery, resin may be used.

2 For a greetings card or bookmark, use heat-seal film for best results. This film can be removed many times to replace straying flowers and when perfect, it is heated with an iron to seal the card. You can also use a normal self-adhesive film, but once applied it cannot be removed.

Greetings card PROJECT

Friends and family love receiving homemade gifts, and this pressed flower card depicting a vase of flowers will be no exception. The flowers, leaves, and stems are sealed in place so that they will not spoil when the card is taken out of the envelope.

YOU WILL NEED

- thick white card or blank greetings card measuring 30 x 40cm (12 x 16in)
- pressed tendrils (sweet pea, bryony, or passion flower)
- milk bottle top or jar lid to hold the glue
- rubber-based glue
- cocktail stick
- 3 or 4 different types of pressed flowers, such as larkspur, buttercups, potentilla (cinquefoil), and melilot (sweet clover)
- tweezers
- 2 different types of pressed leaves, such as alchemilla conjuncta (silver lady's mantle) and potentilla
- small scissors
- pressed grass stems
- self-adhesive or heat-seal film

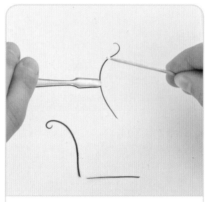

1 Fold the card in half then open it up. Work on the right-hand side of the card. Use the tendrils to create the sides and base of the vase. Apply a very small amount of glue on the back of each tendril using the tip of a cocktail stick and secure in place.

2 Arrange the flowers above the vase using tweezers so that the largest flower is level with the top of the vase. Arrange the flowers until you're happy with the design. Use some half flowers or buds to add interest, then glue the flowers onto the card.

3 Dot leaves in the gaps. If they are thin enough, tuck them under the flowers. Otherwise, cut the leaves and butt them up against the flowers.

4 Cut some pieces of grass to make stems of different lengths. Add the curly tendrils so that the straighter ends appear to go into the vase.

5 Use a piece of grass to create the water line and a few more to suggest a table. Scatter a few damaged or cut petals on the table to represent fallen petals.

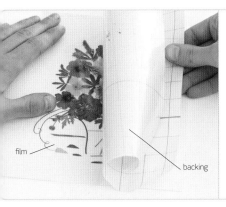

film

backing

6 Cut a piece of film slightly larger all round than the front of the card. Remove the backing and place the film over the flowers. If using self-adhesive film, ensure good contact is made around all the edges of the plant material.

7 If using heat-seal film, place a few layers of cotton fabric on top of the film and press using a warm iron for about 5 seconds: the small air holes will close when sufficient heat has been applied. Do not move the iron during this process. Trim the overlapping edge of the film.

Recycling TECHNIQUES

Natural materials are inexpensive (and often free) and can transform household accessories and ornaments into beautiful objets d'art. You can decorate a box with pine cones, make a pretty picture with shells and driftwood, or create a mosaic with small items such as cloves, seed heads, or even eggshell. Remember to prepare the natural materials carefully before use so that they don't smell or go mouldy over time.

Preparing natural materials

1 Wash out eggshells and boil in a pan of water for a few minutes to sterilize. When cool, peel away the membrane from inside the shell.

2 Soak non-porous items like shells and pebbles in a weak solution of bleach or boil in water to sterilize and kill any bacteria that may cause mould and odours.

3 Dry out pine cones and other porous objects by spreading them on baking parchment on a metal tray. Bake on a low heat for about 30 minutes.

Embossing recycled metal

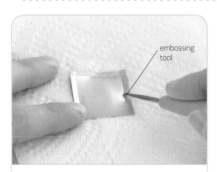

embossing tool

1 Lay a piece of aluminium cut from a drinks can on a pad of folded kitchen paper. Use a fine embossing tool to draw lines on the silver side of the metal. Rub the tip of the tool in a beeswax block to make it easier to draw with.

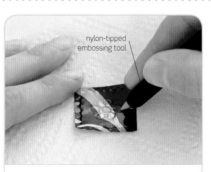

nylon-tipped embossing tool

2 To create a contrast in texture and also to keep the metal flat, turn the panel over and draw on the reverse side. For thicker lines, draw the motif freehand using a nylon-tipped embossing tool.

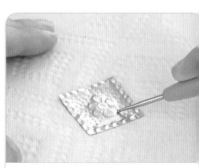

3 Turn the panel over to the right side and finish filling in texture. Use a fine or medium tip to add dots around the motif. You can also add dots or additional lines in a border for a more decorative effect.

Making eggshell mosaic

1 Slightly watered-down PVA glue has a longer drying time: use it to attach pieces of prepared eggshell. Position the pieces using a bamboo skewer, leaving even gaps between them. Attractive eggshells can be stuck face up; stick plain brown hens' eggs face down.

2 Paint the pieces of eggshell with acrylic or watercolour paint for solid colour, or water down the paint for a mottled effect. Leave to dry for 1 hour before grouting.

Grouting the eggshell mosaic

1 Fill the gaps between the pieces of eggshell with grout to create a smooth surface. Mix the grout with a little water to the consistency of thick cream (about 1 part water to 2¾ parts grout). Spoon the grout onto the surface of the mosaic.

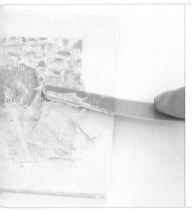

2 Using a flat-edged spatula or palette knife, gently smooth the grout over the mosaic. Work the grout into the crevices, allow to dry for a few minutes, then carefully remove as much of the excess grout as possible with the spatula.

3 Leave to dry for a few more minutes, then wipe clean with a barely damp sponge. Keep rinsing the sponge out in water as you go until the surface is clean but the crevices are still filled with grout. Leave to dry completely, then gently polish the surface with a soft cloth.

Eggshell picture frame PROJECT

This pretty mosaic frame looks so stunning that not many people will guess it's made from ordinary hens' eggs. You can use speckled eggs or even pale blue duck eggs if you can find them, but it's quite easy to colour plain eggshell with watercolour paint. This project is the perfect way to transform that charity shop find. Paint the frame white before you start to give it a neutral finish.

YOU WILL NEED

- pointed craft scissors
- aluminium drinks can
- scrap of paper
- pencil
- flat picture frame, painted white
- kitchen paper
- embossing tools
- strong PVA glue or epoxy resin
- fine and medium paintbrushes
- masking tape
- eggshells
- bamboo skewer
- black watercolour paint
- mosaic grout
- flat-edged spatula or palette knife
- sponge
- soft cloth
- matt acrylic varnish

1 Using craft scissors, carefully pierce an aluminium can and cut around the top and bottom. Cut along the length to create a rectangle. Make a paper template to fit the corners of your frame and use it to cut four squares from the aluminium rectangle.

2 Draw a border on the silver side of the metal squares. Refer to the template on p.60 to draw a heart shape and embellish it with dots. Draw some lines around the border on the reverse side both for decoration and to keep the metal flat.

3 Use a strong PVA glue or epoxy resin to stick the aluminium squares onto the corners of the frame. Wrap masking tape across the corners to hold the squares in place until dry.

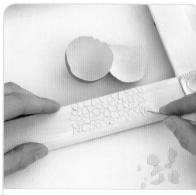

4 Prepare enough eggshells for the size of the frame, following **preparing natural materials** on p.36. Break the eggshells into small pieces and stick to the frame with PVA glue diluted with a little water.

5 Once the glue has dried, mix black watercolour paint with water to make a wash and paint the pieces of eggshell to create a mottled effect. Leave to dry for about 1 hour.

6 Mix some mosaic grout with a little water to make a thick cream. Following the directions for **grouting** on p.37, apply the grout to the mosaic. Leave to dry completely, then buff with a soft cloth. Apply matt acrylic varnish over the mosaic to finish.

Painting furniture TECHNIQUES

Painting furniture is an excellent way to give an old piece a new lease of life, as well as a personal and individual touch. If you're a novice, it's sensible to choose a plain, uncomplicate piece of furniture to start with, and to paint it with a simple design. Once you've mastered th techniques, you can progress to more intricate decoration.

Preparing the furniture

If the furniture is varnished, sand all outer surfaces lightly with medium-grade sandpaper. This roughens the surface so the paint will adhere. Wipe off any dust with a damp cloth.

Priming and painting the furniture

1 Working in the direction of the wood grain and using a large brush, apply two coats of primer undercoat to the outside of the furniture. Use a small brush for hard-to-reach areas. Leave to dry for six hours, then apply two coats of satinwood or eggshell paint to areas that are not to be stencilled.

2 On parts of the furniture that will be stencilled, such as drawers or doors, paint two coats of matt emulsion over the primer undercoat. This provides a good surface for the decoration and will be protected by two coats of clear varnish once the design has been added.

Making a stencil

1 For inspiration, look through interior design magazines and look at wallpaper and fabric designs. Additionally, there is a wide range of copyright-free design books available, which provide a variety of exciting images.

2 Transfer your chosen design to a piece of stencil card. Working on a cutting mat, cut around the design with a scalpel. It's easier to move the stencil around rather than the scalpel. The frame left is the stencil.

Stencilling a two-colour design

1 Fix the stencil firmly in place with masking tape on the item of furniture you are stencilling. Make sure that it is properly centred on the item.

areas for first colour

2 Mask off the areas of the stencil which will be painted in the second colour.

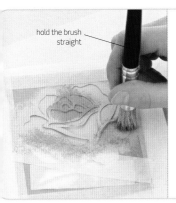

hold the brush straight

3 Artists' acrylic paints work well on wood and can be mixed to create any colour. Dip the tip of a stencil brush in the paint so the brush is fairly dry. Do a test stipple first, then stipple straight up and down through the stencil to prevent the paint seeping underneath. Leave to dry.

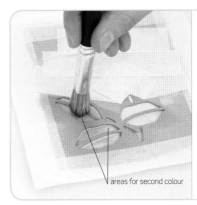

areas for second colour

4 When the first colour is dry, remove the masking tape. Mask off the area that has been stencilled and apply the second colour in the same way, using a clean brush. Remove the masking tape.

Creating stripes and checks

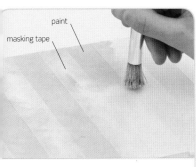

paint

masking tape

1 Masking with tape is a simple way to create crisp stripes. Using a pencil and ruler, mark out the stripes, then apply strips of masking tape within the pencil guidelines. Smooth down the tape to prevent the paint seeping, then stencil as above. Leave to dry.

2 To create checks, remove the tape and apply a second set of tape strips at right angles to the stencilled lines. Stencil in between the tape using a different colour for greater effect.

3 Allow the paint to dry, then peel off the masking tape to reveal the checked design.

Bedside cabinet PROJECT

Transform a plain piece of wooden furniture into an eye-catching focal point. A lick of paint and an attractive design give it a personal and individual look. For a smart, contemporary effect, choose a pale, neutral colour for the background, and a darker neutral for the design. Add new drawer knobs to complement the piece.

YOU WILL NEED

- cabinet
- screwdriver
- medium-grade sandpaper
- cloth
- masking tape
- primer undercoat
- large and medium decorating brushes
- quick-dry satinwood or eggshell paint
- matt emulsion to match the satinwood
- tracing paper
- pencil
- artists' brushes in various sizes
- artists' acrylics or sample pots of paint
- quick-dry clear varnish

1 Remove the knobs and pull out the drawers. Lightly sand all surfaces, including the drawers, then wipe off any dust. Stick masking tape on the sides of the drawers to prevent marking them with paint.

2 Apply primer with a large decorating brush to the body and drawers, painting evenly in the direction of the wood grain. If the paint looks patchy, apply a second coat, allowing two hours' drying time between each coat.

3 Apply two coats of satinwood or eggshell paint to the body of the piece (but not the drawers), allowing six hours between coats. Paint one coat of matching matt emulsion on the drawer fronts.

4 Use a photocopier to enlarge or reduce the template on p.60 (or use your own design) so that it fits the size of the drawers. Transfer onto tracing paper then pencil over the reverse. Secure the tracing paper with masking tape to the drawer fronts with the design the right way round, then pencil over the lines to transfer the design onto the drawers and body. Remove the tracing paper.

5 Use artists' brushes to paint the design on the drawer fronts, not forgetting the stems that continue onto the body of the piece. Use artists' acrylics or sample pots of emulsion.

6 With a medium-size brush, apply two coats of varnish to the drawer fronts to protect them from damage. Use an artists' brush to varnish the painted stems. Fit the drawer knobs.

Tinwork TECHNIQUES

Tin plate is a versatile medium: it's strong, long lasting and can be decorated with a variety of finishes. Large, flat sheets of tin can be acquired by cutting open cooking oil cans and flattening out the metal. If you're painting metal, avoid water-based paints as they tend to flake off. If you prefer a natural finish, a coat of lacquer or Danish oil will protect the surface.

Choosing and cleaning the can

Choose a suitable can. Cans with a ring pull – and in particular sweetcorn cans – are ideal because they have a white lining that helps to reflect the light – perfect if you're **making lanterns** (see pp.46-47). Alternatively, you can use any tin can. Tear off the label and remove any blobs of glue with white spirit.

Packing the can

Before punching holes, you'll need to pack the can to prevent it from denting. Fill it with sand, press the sand down firmly with your fingers, then pour water on top until you can add no more. Place the can in the freezer overnight.

Punching holes in the can

1 Masonry nails are hardened, so they are ideal for punching holes in tin cans. Place the can on a sandbag. To make large holes, punch with a small nail first, then punch in the same place with one or more larger nails to enlarge the hole.

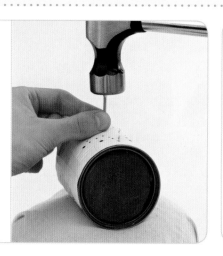

2 If the nail sticks in a hole, use mole grips and a twisting action to remove it.

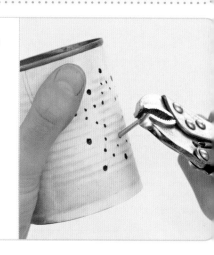

Making wire handles

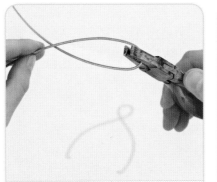

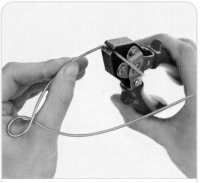

1 To add handles, punch a pair of holes opposite each other 1cm (³⁄₈in) below the top of the can. Once you've emptied the can (see below), cut a piece of coat hanger wire slightly longer than the final handle size.

2 Use ring-bending pliers to make a tight curve in the middle of the length of coat hanger wire. Use your hands to bend the ends into gentle downward curves, using the template on p.61 as a reference.

3 Bend the wire ends at right angles and trim these to about 3mm (¹⁄₈in) with a small pair of bolt cutters. Squeeze the handle to compress it slightly, then fit the ends into the holes in the can – the handle should hold in place by natural spring action.

Emptying the can

When you've finished punching holes, empty the can by placing it in a container and pouring on boiling water. Leave for 10 minutes to allow the ice to melt, then pour out the sand and water. Rinse and dry the can.

Painting the can

1 Fill the can with newspaper to protect the inside and lay sheets of newspaper over your work surface to protect it.

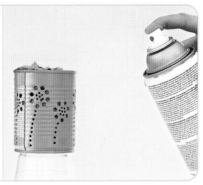

2 Spray the outside of the can evenly with the colour of your choice, then leave to dry for 24 hours. Alternatively, you can brush on an appropriate metal paint or apply a thin coat of oil-based paint.

Tin can lanterns PROJECT

It's remarkable what you can make with rubbish! Here's an attractive way to recycle tin cans into simple lanterns. This project uses small cans, but if you use larger ones, you might find glass jars that fit inside them to protect the candles from the wind. If you don't have any wire coat hangers, 2mm (1/16in) diameter galvanized fencing wire is a good substitute.

YOU WILL NEED

- tin cans
- cloth
- white spirit
- sand
- paper and pencil
- sticky tape
- fabric bag filled with sand
- masonry nails
- hammer
- small mole grips
- wire coat hangers
- small bolt cutters
- ring-bending pliers
- newspaper
- spray paint

1 Remove the label and any blobs of glue from the can. Pack the can with sand, top up with water, and freeze overnight.

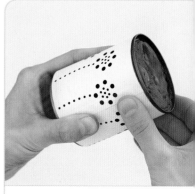

2 Draw your design on a piece of paper to fit the size of the can or photocopy one of the templates on pp.60-61. Tape in place. If you're drawing your own design, ensure that the gap between holes is at least as large as the diameter of each hole.

sandbag

3 Place the can on the sandbag. Punch holes in the can. Place the can in the freezer for about 30 minutes after each 10 minutes of work to ensure the can remains solid. If you're making several lanterns, work on them in rotation.

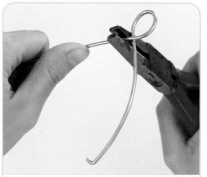

4 Once your design is complete, punch a pair of holes opposite each other 1cm (3/8in) below the top of the can for fitting the handle. Remove the sand. Make a handle out of a 25cm (10in) length of wire, following **making wire handles** on p.45.

5 Fill the can with newspaper and spray-paint it evenly. Make sure you work in a well-ventilated area or outside. Once the can is dry, attach the handle.

Wirework TECHNIQUES

Wire comes in a myriad of types. If you are a beginner, copper wire is very good to work with as it is malleable. Many craft stores stock wire in a range of coloured finishes, and coat hanger wire is ideal when a strong structure is required. Household pliers can be used for wirework, but the serrated jaws can mark soft metals such as copper or aluminium.

Straightening a wire hanger

1 Cut the hanging loop and twisted section from the wire coat hanger using small bolt cutters.

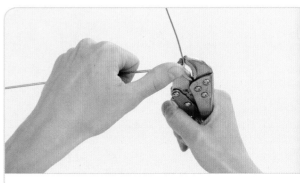

2 Straighten the length you are left with – it may help to use mole grips to straighten the corners.

Straightening lengths of wire

Binding wire together

Shaping wire

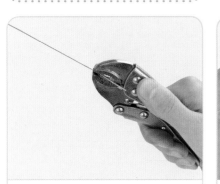

Pulling soft metal wire such as copper or aluminium to straighten it works well. Attach one end to a strong fixing point (a door handle for instance) and hold the other end in mole grips. Pull until the wire is straight.

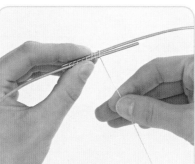

To bind two lengths of coat hanger wire together, overlap the ends by at least 5cm (2in) and wrap medium-gauge wire around the overlap until the ends are held firmly together.

Gentle curves can be bent by hand, but for tighter curves in heavy-gauge wire, use a pair of ring-bending pliers – their smooth jaws do not mark the wire. If you're following a template, have it nearby for reference.

Twisting wires

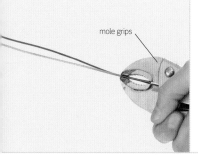

mole grips

1 If you need a long length of twisted wire, bend a length of wire in half, attach it to a strong fixing point (a door handle works well) and lock the two ends in a pair of mole grips.

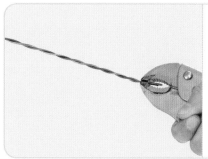

2 Pull the wire taut and turn the mole grips until you have an even twist along the whole length. Cut the wire to remove it from the fixing point.

Joining wires

If you're working with wire and it breaks or runs out, attach another length by making a tiny loop in the end of each wire using round-nose pliers. Link the loops together, and press them closed with mole grips.

Wrapping wire

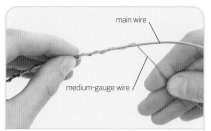

main wire

medium-gauge wire

Cut a length of medium-gauge wire one and a half times the length of the main wire. Curl the end of the medium wire around one end of the main wire, then wrap it around the main wire. Maintain tension so it is wrapped tightly and keep the spacing even.

Making a circular base

Bend a length of wire to form a circle. Overlap the ends by 4cm (1½in). Wrap a short length of medium-gauge wire around the overlap to hold the structure together.

Making a hanging jar

1 Cut a length of medium-gauge wire about 55cm (21½in) long and wrap it once around the jar, just below the lip. Twist the end around the wire to secure.

2 Pull the free end of the wire over to form a handle, then thread it under the loop around the jar. Twist the end to secure it onto the ring. Trim any excess wire.

Making an "S" hook

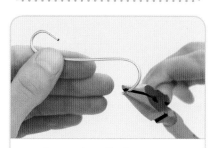

To make an S-shaped hook, curl one end of a 10cm (4in) piece of coat hanger wire using pliers to create a curve and the other end inwards to create a small loop.

Wire heart decoration PROJECT

This wire heart makes a perfect Mother's Day gift or a gift for a close friend. It's fashioned from a wire coat hanger and a handful of mother-of-pearl buttons. If you can't find any suitable buttons, use beads instead.

YOU WILL NEED

- wire coat hanger
- small bolt cutters
- mole grips
- ring-bending pliers
- fine 0.4mm silver-plated wire
- wire cutters
- superglue
- mother-of-pearl buttons

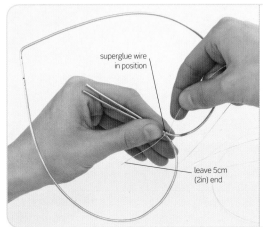

superglue wire in position

leave 5cm (2in) end

1 Cut the hanging loop off the hanger and straighten the hanger. Bend it following the template on p.61, using your hands and ring-bending pliers. Cut a 2.5m (8ft 2in) length of fine wire with wire cutters. At the top of the heart, where the curves meet, join the ends of the coat hanger wire with four of five turns of fine wire. Pull the wire tight, leaving a 5cm (2in) tail. Add a drop of superglue to fix the wire in position and leave to dry.

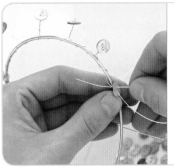

2 With the long end of the fine wire, make two loose turns along about 2cm (³⁄₄in) of the heart, then pull the end of the wire up through one hole in a button and back down through the other hole. Take care not to kink the wire as you pull it through.

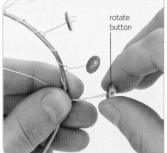

rotate button

3 Hold the button 1.5cm (⁵⁄₈in) from the heart and grip the two pieces of fine wire where they meet the heart. Rotate the button to twist the wire. Make two more turns of the fine wire around the heart, add another button, then repeat all the way round.

4 After the last button, make a couple of turns of the fine wire to return to the starting point. Take the wire through three buttons, adding a turn around the heart each time, then twist the 5cm (2in) tail of wire to finish off. Trim the twisted wire to 5mm (¹⁄₄in) and fix it in place with a small drop of superglue.

5 Cut a 30cm (12in) length of fine wire, bend it in half, and twist, following **twisting wires** on p.49. Form it into a loop. Tuck one end of the loop under the point where the first button was attached to the heart and bend the ends back on themselves. Trim the excess wire and cut off the ends of the wire hanger with small bolt cutters.

6 Fix the other end of the loop to the last button attached to the heart, as in Step 5. Add a button at the mid-point of the loop by threading a short length of thin wire through the button and fix in place by twisting the ends at the back. Trim the ends. Adjust the buttons so that they are arranged neatly around the heart. Add a dab of superglue to the back of each button to fix it in place.

Soap-making TECHNIQUES

The basic technique of soap-making involves melting a soap base and re-moulding it into bars or slabs filled with your own custom scents, colours, and additives. Once you have mastered these basics, you can branch out to create highly decorative soaps using techniques such as layering and embedding. The only limit is your imagination.

Preparing the soap base

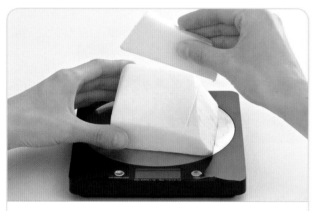

1 Weigh out enough soap base to fill your moulds, allowing a little extra for wastage. Average-sized bars usually require 80 to 100g (3 to 3½oz) of soap. If you're not sure how much soap your mould requires, try cutting a slab to fit it.

2 Use a sharp knife to slice the soap into 2.5cm (1in) chunks. As a rule, the smaller and more regular the pieces, the more quickly and evenly the soap will melt.

Melting the soap base

1 To melt soap on the hob, place it in a heatproof bowl over a pan of simmering water until the soap becomes fully liquid. Stir occasionally but try to avoid generating air bubbles.

2 Small batches of soap can be melted in the microwave. Place the soap in a microwave-proof bowl and heat on full power for a series of 10-second bursts until the soap becomes fully liquid. Never overheat or boil the soap. It only needs to be warm enough to melt.

Colouring the soap

liquid dye

1 Liquid dyes and pigments should be added in tiny increments to the melted soap. Use the tip of a cocktail stick to add colour, one drop at a time.

2 If the colour isn't quite strong enough, add a little more dye and stir until it is fully incorporated into the melted soap.

powdered pigment

3 Add powdered pigment to a small batch of the melted soap and stir to dissolve it. Then incorporate this with the rest of the melted soap, little by little.

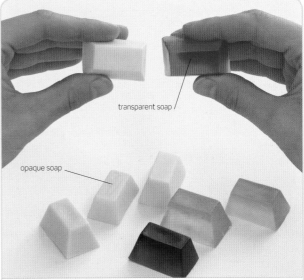

transparent soap

opaque soap

4 For intense, jewel-like colours, combine transparent soap base with liquid dyes or pigment. For flatter, paler shades, use opaque soap base with liquid or powdered colourants.

Scenting the soap

1 Add essential oils and fragrances to the soap just before moulding to minimize evaporation from heat. For small batches, add the oil drop by drop until the aroma is as desired.

fragrance

2 For larger batches, measure out the fragrance into a beaker. Aim for 2 to 3% of the total weight of the soap, or 10 to 15ml (2 to 3tsp) per 500g (1lb 2oz) of soap.

3 When blending scents, experiment with top, middle, and base notes. Putting different combinations of dipped cocktail sticks in a ziplock bag is a good way to play with scent blends.

Enhancing soaps with natural ingredients

1 To add a luxurious, creamy texture to opaque soap, stir in a small portion of a solid moisturising oil such as shea butter while the soap is melting. Do not exceed 5g (⅕oz) per 100g (3½oz) of soap.

shea butter

melted soap

2 For an exfoliating soap, stir in a handful of finely ground oatmeal into the melted soap before moulding. Dried calendula or safflower petals can also be used to create a colourful, mottled texture.

3 For a decorative flourish, place slices of dried citrus fruit in the bottom of the mould and make them adhere by pouring a very thin layer of soap on top. After a minute or two, spritz with rubbing alcohol or surgical spirit then pour in the rest of the soap.

Moulding and storing soap

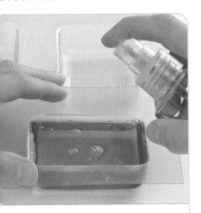

1 Once all the additives are in place, carefully pour the soap into the moulds. It is common for surface bubbles to appear after pouring; these can be dissolved by spritzing immediately with rubbing alcohol or surgical spirit. Leave to set.

2 After several hours, turn the mould upside down and flex each edge gently to release the soap. If the soap is stubborn, place it in the freezer for 15 minutes and try again. Once unmoulded, slabs can be sliced into bars using a knife or metal scraper.

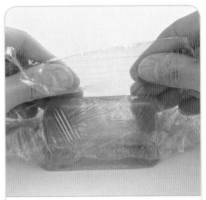

3 If the soap is not for immediate use, store it in clingfilm to prevent its high glycerine content from attracting humidity in the atmosphere and "sweating".

Layering and embedding

1 It is possible to create bars with multiple colours or scents by pouring in separate layers. Spritz the surface of the soap with rubbing alcohol or surgical spirit immediately after pouring, then leave to set. Spritz again before pouring the next layer.

2 Another popular technique is to embed small pieces of contrasting soap into the centre of the soap bars. These may be anything from simple, hand-cut shapes to decorative centrepieces, created with chocolate moulds or cookie cutters.

centrepiece

3 To create the finished bar, chill the centrepieces in the freezer for at least 30 minutes and then work as you would to layer the soap, placing the centrepieces in the middle layer of the soap. Spritz each layer with rubbing alcohol or surgical spirit before pouring the next.

Botanical slab PROJECT

Have you ever wandered around a craft market and admired the array of rough-cut, rustic-looking, natural soaps that are on offer? You too can produce your very own slab of soothing lavender soap that can be cut up into bars and shared with friends. The same approach can be used with a wide range of dried herbs, flower petals, and essential oils.

YOU WILL NEED

- 1 cup of dried lavender buds
- pestle and mortar or food processor
- 650g (1lb 7oz) goat's milk soap base, chopped into small pieces
- heatproof bowl
- saucepan
- metal spoon
- small measuring beaker
- 15ml (3tsp) lavender essential oil
- Tupperware container (approx 12.5 x 18cm/5 x 7in)
- metal scraper or knife

1 Divide the lavender buds into two equal portions. Finely grind one of the portions using a pestle and mortar or a food processor. Set aside.

2 Place the soap pieces in a heatproof bowl over a saucepan of simmering water and heat gently, stirring occasionally with a metal spoon until the soap has melted. Remove from the heat.

3 Add the lavender essential oil and the ground lavender and stir constantly for 1 to 2 minutes. This will help the lavender to remain evenly suspended within the soap. Allow the soap to cool slightly without setting.

4 Pour the mixture into the container. Before the soap starts to form a skin, immediately sprinkle over the unground lavender buds and press gently with your fingers to help them adhere to the surface.

5 Allow to set for several hours before unmoulding and slicing into smaller blocks using a metal scraper or knife.

Clear heart soap PROJECT

This project uses the technique of embedding to capture a heart within a crystal-clear bar of soap. The soap contains a hidden secret as the outer bar is scented with sweet, spicy rosewood essential oil while the heart at the centre is infused with warm vanilla. The heart centrepiece is created using a chocolate mould but you could just as well use a heart-shaped cookie cutter.

YOU WILL NEED

- 4 x 25g (1oz) portions of clear soap base, chopped into small pieces
- electronic scales
- microwave-proof container
- microwave oven
- teaspoon
- ⅛ tsp bleed-proof powdered soap pigment (this project uses Red Lake)
- 1ml (approx 20 drops) pure vanilla extract
- 4cm (1½in) heart-shaped chocolate mould
- small spray bottle containing rubbing alcohol or surgical spirit
- 2ml (approx 40 drops) rosewood essential oil
- 7.5cm (3in) square soap mould

1 Place one portion of soap in a microwave-proof container and heat on full power using a series of 10-second bursts until melted. Add the pigment and stir until fully dissolved. (If the soap starts to set, put it back in the microwave for 10 seconds.)

2 Now stir in the vanilla extract and pour into the heart-shaped mould. Spritz the surface immediately with rubbing alcohol or surgical spirit to remove any bubbles and place in the freezer for at least 30 minutes to set.

3 Meanwhile, melt a second portion of soap. When it is liquid, add 10 to 15 drops of rosewood oil and stir gently to avoid introducing bubbles. Pour into the square mould, spritzing with alcohol to dissolve any bubbles. The soap should fill one-third of the mould. Leave to set for at least 30 minutes.

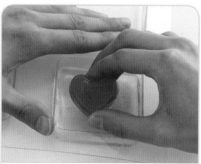

4 Melt another portion of soap and scent with 10 to 15 drops of rosewood. Set aside for 1 to 2 minutes. Pop the heart out of its mould, spritz with alcohol, and place it on the first soap layer. Spritz the entire layer liberally with alcohol then spoon the melted soap around the heart to trap it in place. Leave to set for at least 30 minutes.

5 Repeat Step 3 with the remaining soap. Once it is scented, spritz the previous layer of soap liberally with alcohol to help the final layer to adhere. Pour the melted soap into the mould and spritz one last time to remove any bubbles. Allow to set for several hours before unmoulding.

Templates

Enlarge/decrease
to the required size
on a photocopier

Enlarge/decrease to the required
size on a photocopier

Enlarge by 150% on a photocopier

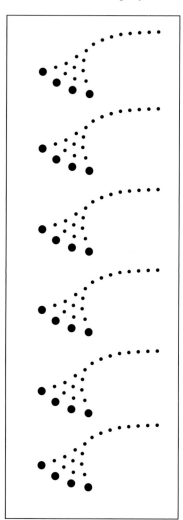

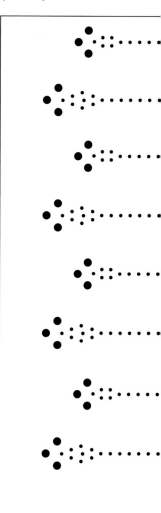

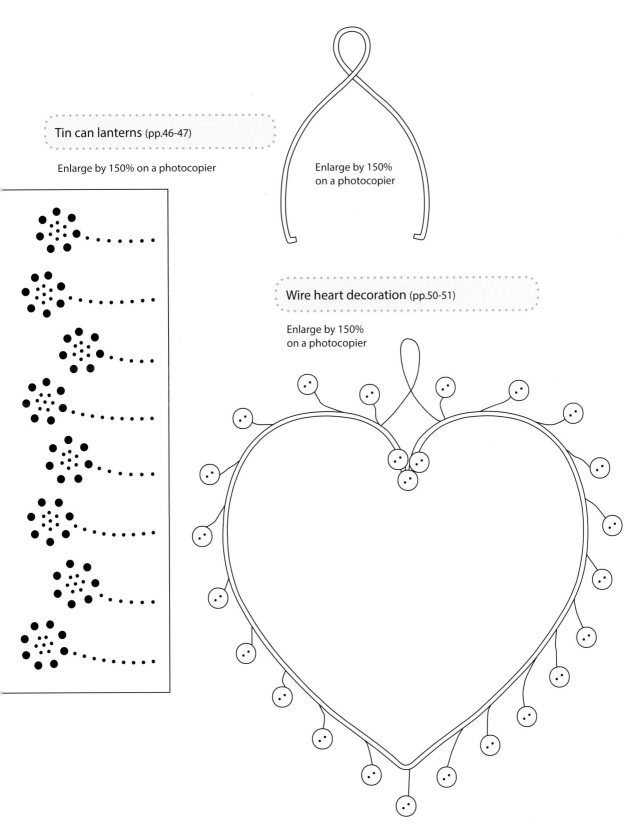

Tin can lanterns (pp.46-47)

Enlarge by 150% on a photocopier

Enlarge by 150%
on a photocopier

Wire heart decoration (pp.50-51)

Enlarge by 150%
on a photocopier

Index

The authors

A talented and dedicated team of crafters, all experts in their field, contributed towards the making of this book.

Michael Ball

tinwork

wirework

Susan Flockhart

botanical slab

clear heart soap

Annemarie O'Sullivan

basketry

Debbie Siniska

rag rugging

Denise Stirrup

pressed flower work

Anne Taylor

furniture painting

Dorothy Wood

recycling

ACKNOWLEDGEMENTS

Dorling Kindersley would like to thank Fiona Corbridge during development, Ira Sharma and Era Chawla for design assistance, Jane Ewart for photography art direction, Ruth Jenkinson for photography, Carly Churchill for hand-modelling and photographic assistance, Meryl Davies for photographic assistance, Hilary Mandleberg for sense-checking, Ria Holland for design assistance, Katie Hardwicke for proofreading, and Marie Lorimer for indexing.